AMAZING PREDATORS

John Townsend

www.raintreepublishers.co.uk
Visit our website to find out
more information about
Raintree books.

To order:

☎ Phone 0845 6044371

📄 Fax +44 (0) 1865 312263

✉ Email myorders@raintreepublishers.co.uk

Customers from outside the UK please telephone +44 1865 312262

Raintree is an imprint of Capstone Global Library Limited,
a company incorporated in England and Wales having its
registered office at 7 Pilgrim Street, London, EC4V 6LB –
Registered company number: 6695582

Text © Capstone Global Library Limited 2013
First published in hardback in 2013
Paperback edition first published in 2014
The moral rights of the proprietor have been asserted.

Edited by Rebecca Rissman, Dan Nunn,
  and Catherine Veitch
Designed by Joanna Hinton-Malivoire
Picture research by Mica Brancic
Production by Victoria Fitzgerald
Originated by Capstone Global Library
Printed and bound in China by CTPS

ISBN 978 1 406 24121 1 (hardback)
16 15 14 13 12
10 9 8 7 6 5 4 3 2 1

ISBN 978 1 406 24128 0 (paperback)
17 16 15 14 13
10 9 8 7 6 5 4 3 2 1

British Library Cataloguing in Publication Data
Townsend, John
Amazing predators. -- (Animal superpowers)
591.5'3-dc23
A full catalogue record for this book is available from the
British Library.

Acknowledgements
We would like to thank the following for permission to
reproduce photographs: Alamy pp. 6 (© WaterFrame),
8 (© A & J Visage); Dr Arthur Anker (UFC, Brazil)
p. 12; FLPA p. 21 (Silvestris Fotoservice); Getty Images
pp. 10 (Peter David), 16 (Digital Vision), 23 (National
Geographic); Nature Picture Library pp. 9 (© Kim Taylor),
11 (© David Shale); Science Photo Library p. 7 (Pascal
Goetgheluck); Shutterstock pp. 4 (© Christos Georghiou),
13 (© John A. Anderson), 14 (© Kjersti Joergensen), 15
(© Marjan Visser Photography), 17 (© bluecrayola), 18
(© Cathy Keifer), 19 (© Pierre-Yves Babelon), 20
(© Susan Flashman), 22 (© Art man), 24 (© Keith Levit),
25 (© Mogens Trolle), 26 (© Kletr), 27 (© Kletr), 29
(© Danomyte); p. 5 (Paul Whitehead).

Cover photograph of a crocodile reproduced with
permission of Shutterstock (© Evlakhov Valeriy). Every
effort has been made to contact copyright holders of
material reproduced in this book. Any omissions will
be rectified in subsequent printings if notice is given
to the publisher.

Some words are shown in bold, **like this.** You can find
out what they mean by looking in the glossary.

Contents

Animals can be supervillains!. 4

Super zap. .6

Super shoot 8

Super trick 10

Super strike 12

Super stun 14

Super scary 16

Super tongue 18

Super snapper 20

Super drinker 22

Super killer 24

Super deadly 26

Quiz: Spot the supervillain! 28

Glossary .30

Find out more 31

Index 32

Animals can be supervillains!

Supervillains in stories have scary superpowers that can do harm. But did you know that some animals also have frightening skills? Read this book to find out which animals use superpowers to frighten their enemies.

Did you know?

The tiny shocking pink dragon millipede has a secret weapon. It can give out a deadly gas.

Super zap

Many animals with supervillain powers live in rivers and oceans. The electric eel can **stun** or kill **predators** with electric shocks. A two and a half metre electric eel is the length of about 12 footballs in a row. It can zap 500 **volts** – enough to kill an adult human.

Did you know?

Scientists use special nets to scoop electric eels up. Otherwise they would get a nasty shock!

Super shoot

Did you know that some fish can shoot? The archerfish is an expert water shooter. It can fire from one and a half metres away and hit its target with its first shot. The jet of water knocks any insect into the river, and the fish gulps it down.

Did you know?

Archerfish can also leap from the water to snatch insects that come too close.

Super trick

The anglerfish lives very deep down in the dark sea. It might look ugly, but the anglerfish attracts its **prey** by using a clever trick. To draw small fish towards its open mouth, it has a light on the end of a spine like a fishing pole. This hangs above its sharp teeth.

light

Super strike

The pistol shrimp can make a noise so loud that it can kill! It has a giant claw that snaps shut and fires a super-hot bubble at **prey**. The bubble bursts louder than a blast from a jet. These "water bullets" can kill small fish.

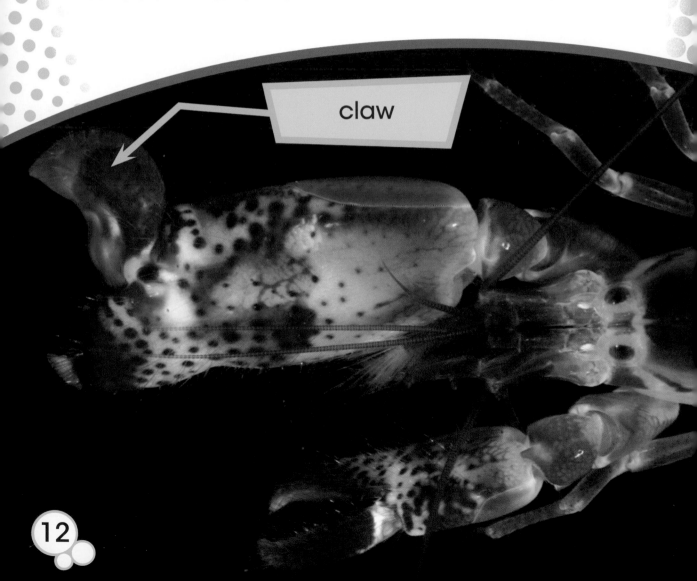

claw

front legs

Did you know?

A mantis shrimp can thump its prey to death with its front legs, with the force and speed of a bullet.

Super stun

Cuttlefish use amazing superpowers to catch their **prey**. As they swim, hover, or walk along the sea floor, they can change colour to look like flashing lights. This **hypnotizes** other fish so that they cannot move. The cuttlefish can gulp them down.

Super scary

Reptile predators use scary superpowers. The spitting cobra can shoot out deadly **venom** with spot-on aim. This killer snake raises its head, spreads out its hood, and sprays blinding venom straight into the eyes of its **prey**. Ouch!

hood

Did you know?

One bite from a king cobra can release enough venom to kill an elephant.

Super tongue

Chameleons are **reptiles** with many superpowers. They can change colour to scare away or hide from **predators**. They can also catch **prey** with their sticky tongues. A chameleon's tongue is longer than its body!

This chameleon has just changed colour – one of its superpowers!

18

tongue

Super snapper

The biggest **reptile** with amazing attacking powers is the super-strong crocodile. The Nile crocodile is a perfect killing machine. Its jaws are strong enough to crush some animals' skulls.

Did you know?

This Saltwater crocodile rolls its **prey** over and over underwater to twist off chunks of meat small enough to swallow. This is called a death roll.

Super drinker

Vampire bats in South America are **mammals** with supervillain powers. They drink blood! After dark, the bats fly from their caves. They can hear the heavy breathing of a sleeping animal and smell its blood from far away.

This vampire bat is drinking blood from a sleeping calf, without the calf even knowing!

Super killer

The lion is known as the king of the beasts. Lions are expert hunters at all times of the day. They are especially good at hunting in the dark because of their excellent night **vision**.

Did you know?

A lioness does most of the hunting. With super-strong jaws and teeth, she quickly kills with one bite to the neck.

Super deadly

Of all the scary **predators**, the anopheles mosquito kills more humans than anything else on the planet. This tiny insect carries the deadly disease malaria. Each year, malaria kills more than one million people in Africa alone.

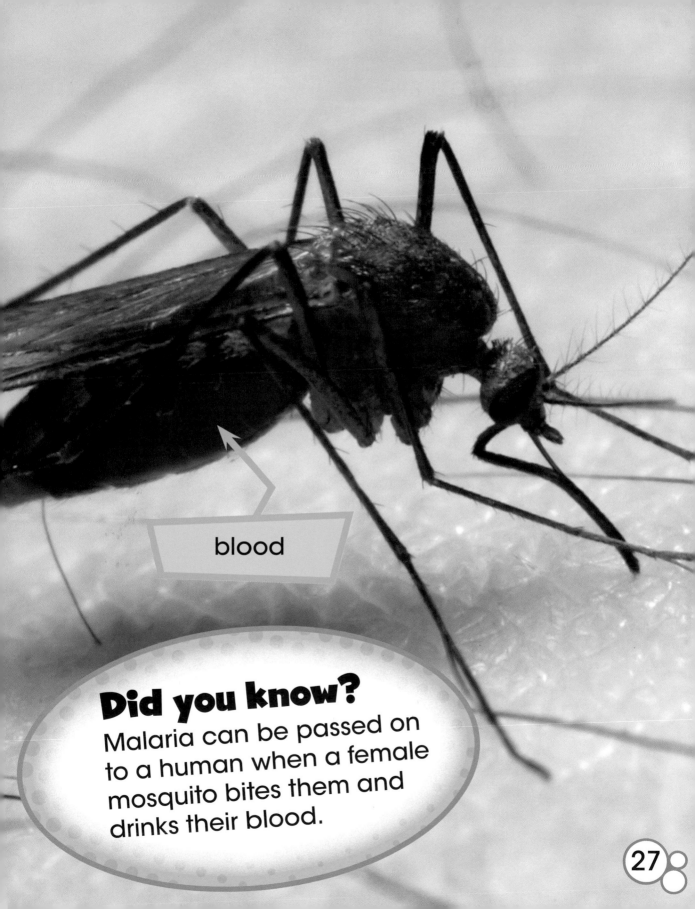

blood

Did you know?
Malaria can be passed on to a human when a female mosquito bites them and drinks their blood.

Quiz: Spot the supervillain!

Test your powers of observation and see if you can spot the supervillain. You can find the answers on page 32 if you are really stuck!

1. Which of these animals can give an electric shock?
a) an eel
b) a lion
c) a shrimp

2. Which of these animals can spit blinding **venom**?
a) a crocodile
b) a cobra
c) a millipede

3. Which of these animals can **stun** with sound?

a) a mosquito

b) a bat

c) a shrimp

4. Which of these animals can strike with a sticky tongue?

a) a chameleon

b) a cuttlefish

c) a lion

5. Which of these animals can catch **prey** with a light?

a) an archerfish

b) an anglerfish

c) an eel

Glossary

hypnotize put someone into a trance or sleep

mammal warm-blooded animal that makes milk for its young

predator animal that hunts other animals

prey animal that is hunted by other animals for food

reptile cold-blooded, air-breathing animal with scaly skin

stun knock unconscious

venom poison that is injected

vision eyesight

volt measure of electrical force

Find out more

Books

Dangerous Animals, Rebecca Gilpin
(Usborne, 2008)

First Encyclopedia of Animals, Paul Dowswell
(Usborne, 2011)

Reptiles, Catriona Clarke (Usborne, 2009)

Websites

animal.discovery.com/videos/fooled-by-nature-archer-fish.html
Watch an archerfish strike on this website.
(You may need to watch an advert before the
archerfish video begins.)

www.yourdiscovery.com/video/natures-perfect-predators-cobra/
Watch a cobra spit venom on this website. (You
may need to watch an advert before the cobra
video begins.)

Index

anglerfish 10–11
archerfish 8–9

blood drinkers 22–23, 27

chameleons 18–19
cobras 16–17
colour changes 15, 18
crocodiles 20–21
cuttlefish 14–15

death rolls 21

electric eels 6–7
electric shocks 6, 7

gases 5

hot bubbles 12
hypnotize 14

jaws 20, 25

lights 10, 11, 14
lions 24–25

malaria 26–27
mammals 22
millipedes 5
mosquitoes 26–27

night vision 24

predators 6, 16, 18, 26
prey 10, 12, 13, 14, 16,
    18, 21

reptiles 16–21

shrimp 12–13
snakes 16–17
stunning with sound 12

tongues, sticky 18, 19

vampire bats 22–23
venom 16, 17

water jets 8

Answers: 1a, 2b, 3c, 4a, 5b.